CLEBERSON EDUARDO DA COSTA

THE CULTURAL INDUSTRY

THE CREATION OF THE MYTH OF THE ENCHANTED PRINCE

Atsoc Editions

We are facing a catastrophe, with regard to the training of men and women:

"Both in so-called rich and so-called poor families, with very few exceptions, women are raised to be self-serving; to marry for money; to marry rich and / or prosperous men, even if they come to surrender for feelings and, men, in another paradoxical and / or different way, to be prejudiced and conservative, that is, promiscuous and polygamous, even if in the condition of said family fathers ...".

CLEBERSON EDUARDO DA COSTA

THE CULTURAL INDUSTRY

THE CREATION OF THE MYTH OF THE ENCHANTED PRINCE

Atsoc Editions

3

ISBN - 9781497459632

Title: THE CULTURAL INDUSTRY AND THE CREATION OF THE MYTH OF THE ENCHANTED PRINCE

1st edition in Portuguese

All rights reserved for this edition: the author

Author

Cleberson Eduardo da Costa

Cover

Atsoc Editions - publisher

Illustration

Atsoc Editions-editorora

Idealization

The author

Graphic Design and Publishing

Cleberson Eduardo da Costa & Atsoc Editions - publisher

International cataloging data at the source of all copyrights

---

C00156A Costa, Cleberson Eduardo Da.

The cultural industry and the creation of the Prince Charming myth. / Cleberson Eduardo da Costa. - Rio de Janeiro: Atsoc Editions - publisher, 2018.

1. Marital relationship; 2. Men and women; 3. Youth and adult education; 4. Sociology; 6. Philosophy; 7. The cultural industry and the creation of the Prince Charming myth. I title.

5

PREFACE

Capital societies, from the development of the Cultural Industry, created two standardized and / or ideal types of men and women, most of the time paradoxical in themselves, such as, for example:

1- Men who, at the same time, are rich, intelligent, muscular, elegant, faithful to their loved ones, affectionate and so-called family fathers, that is, the fictitious representations of said enchanted princes;

2- Women who, at the same time, are said to be of the type of family, well-behaved, faithful, housewives, exemplary mothers and, in the same way, also sexual, hot, sex, seductive slaves, etc.

As it turns out, these two so-called ideals of men and women are paradoxical and therefore, with very rare exceptions, do not exist in the real world.

In the concrete world, outside of fiction, men said to be wealthy (stereotypes of enchanted princes); beautiful, muscular, elegant, etc., with rare exceptions, they are not looking for a single woman for a relationship, but for several, using them as disposable objects or products; and, in that sense, they are also not looking to be parents, etc. That is, men, in these conditions, almost always do not think of having a relationship with a single woman: they, in most cases, are only for many women "loved" and / or idealized as the so-called ideal solution for their lives.

On the other side, of the feminine, the same happens:

> "Many women who seek, at all costs - doing plastics, intensive gym classes, placing silicone prostheses, etc. -, investing massively in the search for beauty, thus trying to enter the said standard of beauty, they do not do so in order to be able to relate to a single

partner, but to be "loved" and / or desired by several (a). "

In addition to using Theodor Adorno's studies on the Cultural Industry, we will also address these issues by understanding how men and women have historically been endocultured from a philosophically critical perspective and analysis, within the sociological and anthropological planes, that is, involving the fragmented and / or fragmentary ideological processes of socialization (Donald Levine) systematized in postmodern Western capitalist societies.

The author

ABOUT THE AUTHOR

Cleberson Eduardo da Costa (more than 100 published books, many of them translated into other languages), born in Rio de Janeiro, graduated in Pedagogy (UERJ - State University of Rio de Janeiro / 1995-1998), Postgraduate in Education (UCAM - Universidade Candido Mendes), Post-graduate student in Philosophy and Human Rights (UCAM - Candido Mendes University), Master and Doctor (free) in Philosophy of knowledge (epistemology) and Clinical Pedagophilosophy (FUNCEC - research, teaching and extension), Researcher, University professor , Specialist in higher education methodology, Degree in Fundamentals, Sociology, Psychology and Philosophy of Education, Didactics, EJA (Youth and adult education) etc.

In addition, he was a special student of the Master of Education (1999-2001 / PROPED / UERJ), enrolled, after approval in a competition, in the disciplines [research seminars] "ESTATUTO FILOSÓFICO" (taught and coordinated by Professor Drª Lilian do Valle); and "EDUCATIONAL POLICIES

IN BRAZIL AND LATIN AMERICA" (taught and coordinated by Professor Dr. Pablo Gentili).

He also studied in the MBA course in Business Management at FUNCEFET / RJ / Região dos Lagos (2003-2005); in the Postgraduate course in Administration and Planning of Education at UERJ (1999-2000); and conducted several free and / or improvement courses in the areas of philosophy and psychoanalysis by different institutions, including FGV (Fundação Getúlio Vargas) and SBPI (Brazilian society of integrated psychoanalysis). From 1998 to 2008, he served as a professor of higher education (Higher Education Institute of UCAM / Cândido Mendes University) on the university campuses of Niterói, Nova Friburgo, Araruama, Rio de Janeiro, Teresópolis, Rio das Ostras, etc.

He participated (in his professional and / or academic intellectual trajectory) in several researches, such as, for example, the UERJ-DEGASE project, related to (EJA) and also in researches centered on political, philosophical and pedagogical problems with renowned teachers, such as Pablo Gentili (UERJ / CLACSO), Cleonice Puggian (UNIGRANRIO), Carla Imenes (UEPG), Cristiane silva Albuquerque (UERJ), Marco Antonio Marinho dos Santos (OCA / RJ) among many others. Currently he is dedicated to university teaching; education research; consultancies related to education, in the sense of improvement, overcoming and human development; academic and multi-organizational lectures and works in the most diverse fields of knowledge.

CONTENT

13

UNIT I

THE CULTURAL INDUSTRY

&

THE CREATION OF THE MYTH OF THE ENCHANTED PRINCE

I CHAPTER - WHAT IS CULTURAL INDUSTRY?

I

The modern age, erected from the 15th and 16th centuries, under humanist and renaissance principles and values, with its scientific and / or Cartesian roots synthesized in its "I think, therefore I am", systematized this rational thought, in opposition to Metaphysics (philosophy) and theology, as the aegis of the construction of a so-called new society.

By rational thinking, we can understand a kind of knowledge that, far from mystical (of religion), mythical (of myths), abstract and / or critically speculative explanations of the world (philosophy), seeks to understand it from the understanding of the laws of nature, in a so-called proven, universally valid way, synthesized in the idea of "to foresee to provide" and / or else "to know to control". In other words, rational scientific thinking seeks to understand the world, the laws of nature and the universe, based on synthetic knowledge "a priori" that, later, in the late 18th century, were synthesized and / or defined by Kant as being specifically "those who are independent of the experience", even if they are reached precisely starting from it (from the experience), that is, from "initial empirical propositions", To summarize, in the words of the philosopher CHAUÍ, Marilena:

> *"Modernity ended a process that philosophy began in Greece: the disenchantment of the world, that is, the passage from myth to reason, from magic to science and logic (...)."*(CHAUÍ, Marilena. Invitation to philosophy. São Paulo: Ática. 200. P. 422-423)

II

However, what must also be said is that the claims of Cartesian science ended up becoming corrupted by becoming merged, for example, with the values of capitalism which, in turn, among other things, always aiming to conquer new markets, he, that same capitalism:

1- These same principles of said scientific knowledge were used as mechanisms to, first, aiming to increase production:

2- Standardize the manufacture of products and / or services and, later, from the second Industrial Revolution, to:

3- Standardize, too, as what is conventionally called globalization:

4- The different cultures;

5- The different people belonging to them, thus also standardizing, aiming at opening new commercial markets:

6- The ways of being, with regard to moral and / or behavioral aspects;

7- The ways of thinking, with regard to the search, not of the truth, but of logical explanations;

8- The ways of acting, with regard to ethical standards;

9- The ways of feeling, with regard to the ways of liking and / or disliking;

10- The ways of seeing, with regard to aesthetic standards and / or what should be seen or considered to be beautiful or made.

This process started with the first industrial revolution, which took place in England at the end of the century. XVIII, where the artisans who, before, dominated all the means and stages of production (beginning, middle and end), became, by the owners of capital, gathered in factories, as proletarians, aiming to increase productivity, performing tasks scientifically standardized, specific, repetitive, that is, losing the knowledge of the whole.

These workers, selling their labor power to the owners of capital, inside the factories, spent practically every day, from 12 to 18 hours, performing mechanical tasks, alienated, receiving, for this, a certain salary.

This process, which soon spread to other countries in the world in more refined scientific forms, was characterized by what was conventionally called Industrial and / or Mercantilist capitalism and, soon after, with the emergence of the so-called Taylorist-Ford productive process in America of the North, at the beginning of the 20th century, of Monopoly capitalism.

Later, with the beginning of the so-called Toyotism phase, that is, with the emergence of a productive process that is no less standardized, but also more flexible because of the use of high technologies, the so-called Global Era was inaugurated, with the so-called financial capitalism. , giving rise to multinational and also transnational companies.

Today, in the so-called global era, this universal standardization of products has reached the point that science, subordinated to the economic power of capitalism, for example, proposes to do research in order to discover specialized techniques and / or methods for the production of flavors, artificial smells, etc., thus enabling the commercial expansion, on a planetary scale, of the so-called large food, beverage, beauty and aesthetic standards industries, involving, for example, not only cosmetics and fragrances, but also the consumption of silicone products, with the aim of changing the anatomical aspects of men and women.

III

Furthermore, in another aspect, but within the same specific universe of the subject that is being dealt with here, in those same postmodern capitalist societies, ideologically, it can be said, industrial processes of cultural massification, alienation of "Civil society", called, by Theodor Adorno, even after the mid-1940s, the Cultural Industry. According to him (Adorno), in the words of TERRA, Lygia et al:

> *"The production, distribution and reception of products broadcast by radio, television and even by major*

21

magazine publishers and Best Sellers were organized in an industrial manner. The goods sold by the cultural industry followed the same processes (standardization, choice and target audience, simplification, programmed obsolescence) as those produced by other segments of the industry. (TERRA, Lygia et. Al. Connections: studies of general and Brazilian geography. São Paulo: Moderna, 2010. P. 16)

In other words, what is meant is that "The cultural industry, in the so-called globalized world in which we live today, is linked to the idea of:

1- Universal standardization and / or:

2- Massification of cultural patterns, these being placed as commercial products to be consumed, as an information product, by those who wish and can pay for them.

In this cultural industry, which, in summary, is composed of:

1- From movies,

2- Reading,

3- Magazines,

4- Newspapers,

5- Music CDs, etc., are also placed, as a form of merchandising and / or Marketing strategies of large multinational and transnational companies, note:

6- "A new idealized and standardized type of being", specific to each respective age group of citizens, in them only defined as the same as public-consumer and / or potential consumers. And, also, in the same way, being standardized, for example:

7- What to eat,

8- Who to date and / or marry,

9- What kind of car should you buy, etc., thus establishing a kind of:

10- Dictatorships of fashion, beauty etc. on a global scale.

III

This entire ideological process of capital has led to the formation (as a kind of standardized universal culture) and / or the construction of new programmable psychosocial beings at each strategic change in capitalism's market.

Still in the perspective of Theodor Adorno, referring to this so-called Cultural Industry, which the capitalists often place under the so-called "innocent face of said simple entertainment", wrote TERRA, Lygia et al:

> *"The consequences of this consumer submission to the power of the big entertainment industries affect both the politics of society and the psychology of people."*(TERRA, Lygia et. Al. Connections: studies of general and Brazilian geography. São Paulo: Moderna, 2010. P. 16)

The philosopher Marilena CHAUÍ, in her book "Invitation to Philosophy", critically analyzing

Theodor Adorno's concepts of "Cultural Industry", in the light of Postmodernity, wrote:

> "Beginning with the second industrial revolution in the 19th century and continuing in what is now called a post-industrial or post-modern society (started in the 1970s), the arts were subjected to a new servitude: the rules of the capitalist market and the ideology of the cultural industry, based on the idea and practice of consuming cultural products manufactured in series. " (CHAUÍ, Marilena. Invitation to philosophy. São Paulo: Ática. 200. P. 422-423)

Both Theodor Adorno and Lygia Terra et AL and Marilena Chauí are specifically talking about the fragmented and / or fragmented (alienated) socialization processes, also conceptualized by sociologist Donald Levine, in which individuals, today, in contemporary and / or post-Western societies modern capitalists are being subjected, automatically, on a daily basis. In other words, the socialization processes, today, which take place in a fragmented and / or fragmentary manner, no longer form citizens, but potential consumers according to their specific age groups when, for example, what is defined and / or what it should be:

1- Young fashion;
2- Kids Fashion;
3- Teenage fashion;
4- Teen fashion etc. and, following, at the same pace:
5- The so-called different musical styles,
6- Living, etc., created by the most varied and multiple global consumer industries, built by the dictatorships of multinational and / or transnational companies that operate globally.

In the UN / UNDP 2004 "human development report", for example, talking about these processes of "socialization of young people and adults", which, now, in these societies has taken place not only through the family, the school and the other concrete and / or traditional social groups of social interaction and / or socialization of individuals, but also in a fragmented, fragmentary and / or alienated way through this so-called Cultural Industry, it was informatively written:

> *"The consumption patterns are, today, worldwide. Market research has identified a "world elite", a world middle class that follows the same style of consumption and prefers global brands. The most impressive are the "world teenagers", who inhabit the world space, with a single world pop culture, absorbing the same videos and the same music, providing a huge market for branded sneakers, t-shirts and jeans. "* (Human development report - New York: UNDP / UN. 2004. P. 87)

II CHAPTER - THE CULTURAL INDUSTRY AND THE CREATION OF THE MYTH OF THE ENCHANTED PRINCE

Based on the theme discussed in the previous chapter, in a macro sense, making an analogy with all the other formative (deformative) processes that have occurred through the Cultural Industry, it can be said that they are given, also as forms of market reproduction , the creation of new postmodern myths such as, for example:

1- Those of the so-called "Prince Charming", which was systematized with the stories of Romeo and Juliet, Rapunzel, etc., and, in the present day:
2- Through the most varied and, at the same time, similar so-called love stories, involving:
3- The so-called heartthrobs of novels and / or films of Hollywood, whose main personages or protagonists and antagonists are:
4- Skinny girls,

5- Blondes, etc.,

6- Barbie stereotypes and, in the case of men:

7- Embodied in the financial, aesthetic-athletic standards of the princes of fairy tales, etc., without forgetting here to mention the peculiar dictatorships of their plots (always or almost always with happy ends).

In other words, today, at the dawn of the 21st century, novels, books, films, etc., not only European and North American - not just romantic ones - bring with them these standardized and universalized ideas of women who, for living dreaming of meeting, in real life, with their so-called enchanted princes, until they find them, they live sad and, soon after, finding them, they start to live "happily ever after".

There is, thus, culturally, through this Cultural Industry, under the massive and mass reproduction of these stories of fairy tales, by different media, the same thing to be emphasized:

1- *"An imposition not only of ways of being, feeling and existing, but also:*
2- *Of aesthetic standards considered essential when women and men seek out their emotional partners:*
3- *Be it just for sexual involvement without compromises;*
4- *Whether for the search for a marital relationship.*

In the case of men, these films, and even drawings, reproduce the macho and prejudiced ideas that have long been part of their training. For example:

> *"When these films are just about having fun with young people and / or adults, the women who are considered ideal are those:*
>
> 1- *Of the "extravagant" type, sex and / or said hot girls;*
> 2- *Those that they, the men, dream of spending just one or a few nights with them fulfilling their sexual fantasies and nothing more.*

On the other hand:

> "When the films portray weddings, women are usually those like:
>
> 1- *Behaved and / or said of families;*
> 2- *Dressed in their austere or sober clothes.*

Even in the well-known film "called a beautiful woman", the prostitute, played by Julia Roberts, has the appearance of a well-behaved, sensitive, polite and family-oriented woman.

In other words, the idea arises that she "is" as a prostitute and not that she, her character, is in fact and / or essentially "be" one.

In other words, what is meant is that, with regard to the so-called women of the family, the possible ideal affective pairs for marriage are placed for them:

> *"They are placed, in the same way, almost always:*

1- Men, in addition to "standardized" so-called beautiful, also:
2- Rich and / or very successful, faithful, educated, etc.

On the other hand, in films that involve only fun or entertainment:

"Men placed as ideal by them and / or for them:

1- They are those who are like rich people,
2- Well born and / or little daddy's children,
3- Living in mansions and / or on board their powerful cars, sports bikes or yachts.

The philosopher Marilena Chauí, also discussing the problem regarding the concept of cultural industry created by Theodor Adorno and, in the same way, theorizing about the catastrophic power of alienation caused by her to individuals in capitalist societies, wrote to us:

The cultural industry sells culture:

1- *To sell it you must seduce and please the consumer.*
2- *To seduce him, please him, he cannot shock, provoke, make him think. Make him have new information that disturbs him, but:*
3- *It must return to him, with a new appearance, what he already knows, what he has already seen, he has already done. That is:*
4- *The average is what the cultural industry returns with a new look.* (Text adapted from CHAUÍ, Marilena. Invitation to philosophy. São Paulo: Ática. 200. P. 422-423)

In other words, the cultural industry sells what it says is culture and, in that sense, as culture, according to the bases of Anthropology, they are the same as ways of life and manifestations of any people and / or any social group, it can also be

33

said that, in order to be able to sell it, it is necessary not only to seduce and please the consumer, but also:

1- Create an alienated consumer even before creating his own products, he, that same consumer, believing himself hyperconscious:
2- Will be predisposed to want and / or wish to consume.

This is, today, the Cultural Industry, not only through market research:

1- It seeks to discover what people need in order to be able to create their cultural products so that they can be consumed by them. She, the Cultural Industry, today, in the postmodern era:
2- First, it also creates the consumer of products that it has not yet created, that is, it "creates consumer desires", only then to create its specific products and / or services so that they can then be consumed by them.

Having clarified these first points, but also seeking to complement them and continue our propositions, in the next chapter, by revealing data from an important research carried out with boys and girls in elementary school regarding these fragmented and / or fragmentary processes of socialization (alienation) that start in the family, even before school, we will try to deepen these axioms about the idea of "socialization by fragments", where "the other" (different), in a systematic way, has been socially transformed "in the same" (be standardized) through the dictatorship of the Cultural Industry.

That is, through this imposition of consumption values, which end up translating and / or giving rise to alienated choices from affective and / or sexual couples for dating and / or marriage relationships between men and women in these same post-capitalist societies. during youth and / or adult life.

III CHAPTER - THE SYSTEMATIZATION OF THE IDEAL OF THE MYTH OF THE ENCHANTED PRINCE: The fragmented and / or fragmentary socialization processes present in postmodern capitalist societies.

In a recent survey of male and female students in the first grades of primary education in public and private schools in the state of Rio de Janeiro, the results of which were reported by a major TV station in the first months of 2013 , there was a serious problem of formation and / or socialization of children belonging to the first and second grades:

> *"The psychosocial development based on the internalization, by children, of stereotypes involving certain aesthetic standards imposed by the cultural and consumption dictatorship coming from the means of communication and / or information present in postmodern capitalist societies."*

The research took place as follows:

The children (from different educational institutions, public and private, from the capital and the countryside) were randomly placed, in groups of ten to twenty students, placed in three situations:

1- Firstly, to watch a drawing, the plot of which involved a love story between a prince and a princess of European origin, whose characters, with Nordic features, were white and blond with green or blue eyes.

2- Secondly, without intervals, these same children, right after, watched another drawing, whose plot was the same, that is, it involved a love story between a prince and a princess. However, in this second drawing given to students, the characters had non-white skin and brown or black hair and eyes.

At the end, after having watched the drawings, the children received in their hands posters of the characters of the same ones they had already seen (of the two drawings) and were asked to answer, individually, in another room (in which they were randomly invited to enter , no longer turning to the same group of children to whom they had left), the following questions:

1- Which of the drawings spoke of love stories between princes and princesses?
2- Which of the cartoon characters would they like to be? If this were possible, including the color of the skin, hair, eyes, etc .;
3- Which characters, involving the two drawings, did they consider to be beautiful?

As was not to be expected, although the premises were shown to be relevant in this direction, more than 90% of the responses of students, who were even videotaped, revealed that the majority of children, both in public and private schools:

1- He only considered the first drawing, the one of Nordic essence, whose characters had light skins, blond hair and blue or green eyes, as that of a love story between prince and princess;

2- They would just like to be the characters, male for boys and female for girls, representative of that same film;

3- They only considered the characters and / or the characters in that same film beautiful and / or beautiful.

Note that, in order to avoid negatively influencing children, they were not asked, for example, which of the characters they considered ugly.

Upon learning of the data of this research, the need immediately came to mind to take them to the light of a philosophical proposition that could allow us to understand it (the research) within a context and a historical perspective, post-industrial revolution , involving the development of the values of capitalism itself, characterized and fostered by the development of the so-called, by Theodor Adorno, Cultural Industry, given that, before the socialization given at school, children naturally go through another socialization process, the primary school, which, before, occurred more specifically in the family and, today, has also occurred through the mainstream media (especially through so-called children's programs on TVs, DVDs, etc.).

These questions led us to reflect, for example, on the data of the same, comparing them, through a critical theoretical analysis, with the modes of fragmented and / or fragmentary socialization recommended by the American sociologist Donald Levine, developed in the first chapter of his book, called "Visions of the sociological tradition", in which, according to him, today, in the midst of the postmodern era, this process of socialization has been systematically taking place, that is, making individuals, through him, in a alienated, develop, in themselves, certain ways of being, acting, feeling and thinking standardized, specialized and /

or fragments, as if the same, individuals, as the "other", the "different", were being globally transformed into "the same", that is, losing their own identities when being socialized.Take, for example, what he, Donald Levine tells us:

> *"Socialization is increasingly taking place in fragments:*
>
> 1- *Television dumps images and people zap from channel to channel.*
> 2- *Reading books is replaced by reading abstracts or reviews published in periodicals, when not just phrases and paragraphs in weekly magazines.*
> 3- *Computers present news and information as if they are all the same and have the same importance.*
> 4- *Parents deliver their children to schools and believe that they are educating them.*
> 5- *Students have a reduced ability to argue reasonably and do not have a procedural historical view of what is happening.* (In: TOMAZI, Nelson Dacio. Sociology. São Paulo: Saraiva, 2010. P. 22)

In this way, we were struck by the way not only how children, but also how young people and adults, albeit unconsciously, in different time-spaces of social life, have been following certain pre-established behavioral and psychosocial patterns in time to seek to get involved with their affective and / or sexual peers in large cities.

In the case of women, for example, it was revealed that, socially, they are placed in their psyches, through these fragmented processes of socialization, some principles and values that make them, even if unconsciously, create and / or sustain the idea and / or the stereotype of the search for the prince charming, in his effective and / or sexual relationships, as being a precondition for them to be happy and, therefore, all those men who are not part of him, of these standards, besides of being conceived as not being beautiful and / or ugly, they are also placed out of the list of men under whom one could have some kind of more serious and / or lasting relationship, culminating in marriage, for example.

What is meant is that, just as men, being raised to be sexist and prejudiced, they create their so-called patterns of women said to be able to marry and women said to only be able to stay and / or else to catch, women, also, albeit unconsciously, they do the same, although there are qualitative differences between them in the definition of these same patterns caused by a different form of socialization.

The problem, in this sense, is given precisely there, in this fragmentary process of socialization. In other words, many women in these capitalist societies, alienatedly, project their dreams of marital happiness in a type of ideal man, that is, that does not exist in the concrete world, but only:

1- In the world of fiction;
2- In the world of fairy tales;

3- In the world of love stories with happy ending to films, etc. and, therefore, when they are not eternally single because they cannot find that rich, blond, tall, loving, faithful and perfect prince:

4- They marry types that they would like to turn into ideals, not loving them as they really are, however, feeling, consequently, some time later, how it could not be different:

5- Frustrated,

6- Fooled,

7- Betrayed, claiming to have married frogs and not their idealized and / or dreamed princes.

That is, in the marital separations, they, the women, in the great majority of times, besides saying they have discovered a frog in the prince's place, they also accuse their now "ex" spouses and / or sexual and / or affective partners:

1- To have deceived them;

2- That they pretended to be the princes they never really were.

It is not being said that, in these cases, women are always wrong. In fact, it must be thought that this problem of frustrations occurs from a kind of codependency. That is, it is being said that:

> *"There are only those men who seek, rationally, to pretend to be princes because there are women - and there are many - who idealize meeting these types of men".*

In other words, without wanting to appear to defend men here, it can be said that the reason why, deliberately, some men, in order to want to conquer some so-called beautiful women, pass themselves off as princes, insofar as in which, some of them, after so much failure in their conquests, come to discover, for example:

1- That they, many women, due to the way they are socialized, for their sexual, affective and / or marital relations:
2- Idealize some specific types of men; and not others.

However, what is meant is that women, since the first socialization, given this in the family, followed by these other fragmentary socialization processes that follow from school, develop in themselves ways of being, of feeling , to think and, in the specific case of the choices of their affective, sexual and / or marital partners, also incorporating patterns said to be adequate or not so that they may or may not be happy in this area.

Within these principles and values, that is, because they are socialized in capitalist societies, where everything has a specific value, feelings and people also become (like goods arranged on a supermarket shelf, for example) objects that may or may not be consumed. . Therefore:

1- In the same way that certain women buy certain types of products, and not others,
2- They also act alienated under certain standards, for example:
3- When seeking their affective and / or sexual peers, aiming at dating and / or marriage, in socially predetermined ways.

IV CHAPTER - PRINCIPLES AND VALUES UNDER WHICH MEN AND WOMEN HAVE BEEN SOCIALIZED IN POST-MODERN CAPITALIST SOCIETIES

The way men and women have been socialized in postmodern societies has an intrinsic relationship with the systematization, in those same societies, of capitalist ethics, based on its principles of "commodification" of all things, be they material and / or immaterial, as in the case of the body and feelings, respectively.

In fact, men are educated to use and change female pairs as they change clothes and cars, following a process of "programmed obsolescence" (incessant search for novelties), where the meaning of life is synthesized in being able to consume and own things. And, in this sense, also translated as being able to satisfy their respective sexual needs, as, for example, in wanting to possess without being possessed, and / or to consume without being consumed, as if that, in fact, were possible.

In the case of women and, even in the case of men, they have become, for each other, in many cases, not only objects of consumption and desire, but also products, when they, for example, get involved with rich men in order to to satisfy their consumption needs and, when they meet them, aiming only at sex, even if directly and / or indirectly (even unconsciously in the case of both). That is, whether they like it or not, they are involved in a game of consumption, of losing and winning, but that, in fact, there are no winners, since, humanly, everyone leaves this process worse than when they entered it , that is:

1- Unhappy and / or bitter - in the case of both;
2- With low esteem - in the case of women;
3- Feeling used - in the case of women;

4- Unable to trust their partners and establish lasting relationships - in the case of both;

It would be no exaggeration to say that, in postmodern capitalist societies, sincere love between men and women has become not only a product, but a product that many seek, knowing, at the same time, that it does not exist and / or that, if it exists, it has, for a long time, been scarce in the market for men and women called quality.

Women, historically, and even today, with very few exceptions, are raised essentially differently from men, although, in postmodern societies, the feminist movement has led many to want to be, also, in the sense of channeling, of polygamy and the so-called "pegação", equal to men, exactly in what, ethically and morally, they have in themselves - in my view -, culturally, of worse and lesser value. In other words, it can and must be said that women, on the basis of feminism, should rather fight for equal rights and conditions equal to men, whether in the world of work and / or in any other area and / or social sphere.

However, the radical feminist foundations that preach that women must be "equal" to men in terms of debauchery and polygamy need, first of all, in my view, to be rethought.

Women, when born, unlike men, have their genitals protected and, why not say, hidden not only from the public view - unlike the case of the penis, in relation to men - but also from their own family members and, in many cases, of the father himself, the vision of his vagina being exclusive to that of the female sex and, in most cases, only that of his mother and / or that mother, who directly takes care of her.

In this sense, unlike the word "penis", called "piru" in popular language, the word "vagina" in the popular language "xereca", even today, in many and often, is not even pronounced in the ears of girl, within many families, during her childhood. It is not being said that this has to be different. In other words, it is not being said that girls have to be raised by showing their vaginas publicly, in order to assert their femininities, as men do with their penises. What is meant is that the way girls have been brought up, up to the present day, actually favors their ignorance of their own bodies and also their sexualities.

While men grow up learning to touch themselves and to know their genitals, besides being constantly impelled to speak his name and even hear him in the family and among men, as a mechanism for the formation of their masculinity, women, while on the contrary, they are prohibited, even if not directly, from pronouncing the name of theirs in childhood.

There are no known cases of girls who, along with their mother, her friends and those of their mother, have been driven, by the mother herself and / or by a group of adult women, to have to show, in front of other women and men your vagina, touching it with your hand, as a symbol and / or synonym for the affirmation of your femininity. Quite the contrary, if such a girl, as a child, at least was and, today, is caught scratching or touching herself near her vagina, she would certainly hear and will still hear: "Girl, take your hand away. Stop moving right there ... You shouldn't move in that place ... "

While men grow up talking about sex and sexuality both at home and on the street, among colleagues, women since childhood grow as an alien in relation to this subject, even though, in contemporary societies, due to technological advances, the possibilities of information have been expanded, but in a fragmented way, as we saw in the previous chapter, on sexuality, through TV, films, soap operas, etc. Even at school, which should be a space for learning and discussion, the topic of sexuality, in terms of not only the knowledge of boys, but also that of girls, still remains a taboo. In some cases, which are not uncommon, the girls only took and take the little knowledge of their bodies and organs from biology classes. Even so, they did not allow them and, even today, in many schools, they do not allow the development of plausible and necessary knowledge for the broad development, by the girls, in this area.

What is meant is that, while men arrived and arrive in adolescence and youth having even masturbated and / or even had an early sexual experience, many women, given to this ignorance, in an attempt to discover something in this sense, they end up losing their virginity and, in many cases, without feeling any satisfaction or pleasure in it, which often results in an early pregnancy.

In another way, while men enter youth and adult life separating emotion from sexuality, women, for not knowing what emotion and sexuality are, in this phase, end up making an intrinsic relationship between both, believing that men , when they have sex with them, before the said marriage, they are also moved, like them, by some kind of feeling.

In adolescence and youth, in many cases, women do not relate sexually by instinctive impulse only, but also because they fall in love and associate feeling with sex, which, for men, differently, almost always, has none. intrinsic relationship.

V CHAPTER - WOMEN ARE "EDUCATED" TO MARRY RICH AND / OR PROSPEROUS MEN AND, MEN, TO BE CHAMPAGNE AND / OR POLYGAMICS (EVEN THAT IN THE CONDITION OF SUCH FAMILY PARENTS).

Women, unlike men, since childhood, also with very rare exceptions, are created to marry and / or have relationships with men who are considered wealthy and / or prosperous, even though some come from families of poor and poor people. / or socially excluded.

In other words, both in the world of the rich and the poor, women are raised, with rare exceptions, to marry rich men. However, in the case of men, they are only required by their social group, even today, to marry beautiful women and, at the same time, to be of the "family" type, that is, in addition to many other things , who have had no or almost no previous sexual experience.

In fact, we are facing a family catastrophe, with regard to the training of men and women:

> "Both in so-called rich and so-called poor families, with very few exceptions, women are created to be self-serving, to marry for money, to marry wealthy and / or prosperous men, even if they will give themselves up for feelings and, men, in another paradoxical or different way, to be prejudiced, conservative, promiscuous and / or polygamous ", even though so-called family fathers. (my emphasis)

In the case of young women, directly and indirectly, consciously or not, it is said, in families, with rare exceptions, that:

> "If the woman gives herself, even if she has feelings or not, choose the man because of the possessions that he or his family has or is supposed to have ..."(emphasis added)

Therefore, when she, this young woman, finds this boy of possessions and surrenders to him, aiming for something more, she does not know that this boy of possessions, unlike her, was "trained / trained" not to value her precisely because , before the wedding and, easily, she, wishing for something more, like many others, deluded, gave herself to him. Until this girl / woman can understand this paradox, it is, as they say, more "round" than the wheel of an old peddler's car and, even worse:

> *"With her image, before her social group, before men, destroyed and / or being called by them an easy woman and, by other women, a slut".*(emphasis added)

In many cases, these women end up, in that sense, disillusioned with life, going into prostitution and / or joining together, already full of children from different parents, with older men, with those they, in their youth, never they did not even dream for their lives: that is, they end up, with rare exceptions, ending up with those men who, far from being the "kittens", were also those who were far from being considered, in youth, by other girls and, for her Don Juan.

In fact, in both cases, both in the education of men and in that of women, if that can be called education, in the poor or rich, with regard to sexuality and / or affective and / or marital relationships, parents or guardians are wrong in their education, and these, together with the mercantilist values of capitalism, are primarily responsible for this human catastrophe, that is: for this relationship of consumption and sale of body and soul, even if indirectly , socially speaking. In other words, with rare exceptions, men are created to:

1- Being scoundrels,
2- Chickens and / or polygamous, although in the condition of said parents.

And, women, also with rare exceptions, to:

1- Being self-serving; and / or to:

2- Marry wealthy and / or prosperous men.

However, men, at the same time, are not only sexist, but some may think:

> *"They are conservative when it comes to family and, in the same way, prejudiced, when it comes to dating and / or marriage."*(emphasis added)

In other words, at the same time that men praise polygamy, with regard to the art of "making out", centered on conquering the greatest number of women possible, with zero or the minimum of feelings nourished in this process, they are also not they marry women who, wanting to be like them, also act like this and, moreover, show interest.

In other words, men seek all kinds of women, said to be easy or difficult, but they do not go out with them in search of marriage or something else, but just fun and entertainment, while these women often give themselves to them precisely for be in search of that "something else".

VI - PRELIMINARY CONCLUSION

All those who, voluntarily and / or involuntarily end up falling within the said standards of beauty and / or aesthetics defined by the cultural industry, naturally also become, as products, objects of consumption for everyone else, inside or outside the standard and in this sense, they are also treated as disposable human beings.

Men and women who meet these standards, psychosocially, are also placed, albeit unconsciously, only to be desired as objects of consumption. This may explain why there is, in these societies, an infinity of men and women who are, in the popular saying "running hand in hand", in search of their so-called peers and / or ideal partners. In other words:

"Men (the stereotypical princes), in postmodern capitalist societies, are trained to want women who

are said to be easy, said to be sexually experienced, in order to fulfill all their sexual aspirations with them."

However, when it comes to getting married, they prefer those who have had no and / or even said very few sexual experiences and, moreover, who demonstrate being with them, not for what they have or for the money they are supposed to have, but for the feelings . Even today, what many are unaware of is that the prejudice of men in relation to the few sexual experiences on the part of women is precisely linked to the question of penis size and the question of virginity, referring to the establishment, in his mind, of two myths (untruths), respectively, namely:

1- Among men there is a myth that the woman who, supposedly, has had many sexual experiences, ends up having the "enlarged" vagina, exhausted beyond measure, always feeling the desire to continue with these experiences, in an incessant search for a big penis that it satisfies her, nevertheless she is never fully satisfied, even after being married, which will lead her, supposedly, as they think, to commit possible adultery;

2- Among men, the idea or myth is also widespread that the man with whom the woman loses her virginity is never totally forgotten by her and that, even, he has eternal powers of seduction over her.

These two (myths), not only for men (of the princes type), with rare exceptions, are the ones that prevent them from even considering the possibility of marrying the women they only "get", especially those in which he and your friends have taken it too. That is, in this specific case, with rare exceptions, men do not marry women who have already gone out with their friends and / or who are said to be spoken badly among them. They even go out with them too, but never looking for bigger commitments. Even in cases where one does everything to go out with the other's so-called girlfriend, the man also does not have the pretension of something more serious with her, since, for him, both women who cheat as much as women do. women who have, over a period of time, many partners, even without betraying any of them, are not worthy of a serious and lasting relationship.

Generally these women that men (not just princes) do not marry, end up becoming said single mothers, with two or more children of different parents, given that those who use them only as objects, often do not also assume the children that they do in them. This is:

> *These women, when they find a partner who really wants to join them, end up being those who are older in relation to them and who, in their youth, became frustrated by not being*

able, for some reason, to become stallions and / or the so-called Don Juan. (my emphasis)

ANNEX I
THE DIFFERENT

I - THE DIFFERENT, UGLY AND / OR EXCLUSIVE BEAUTIFUL

I

The different are those who, in postmodern capitalist societies - and the vast majority - are outside the aesthetic dictatorial standards of what the Cultural Industry's consumption policy systematizes as being said universal standards of beauty. They, these different ones, are real, concrete men and / or women, different from those of fiction. Different, in this sense, it is not, in fact, who, or the one who, for whatever reason and / or deliberate will, intends to be or be:

1- To be different is to be what you are, as a singular entity;

2- To be different is to be ugly, beautiful and / or a unique, exclusive beautiful, outside the universal and / or global aesthetic standards of beauty imposed by the consumer industry of capitalism. That is, stress:

> "The one who pretends to be different, ugly and / or" exclusive beautiful "is only the imitator of a different being, an ugly and / or a beautiful exclusive, but never, in fact, a different being, ugly and / or beautiful exclusive ... "

Different, ugly and / or exclusive beautiful is everyone who, although unaware of their difference, ugliness and / or exclusive beauty, contributes, in some way, to the space-time where it is supposed to be allocated, as a body called foreign :

1- Don't lose your enriching potential;

2- Do not miss the possibility of being able to be glimpsed from another angle, another way or way of seeing;

3- Do not lose the possibility of being taken, as a social interaction, for a space-time of dialogues, as a way to abhor violence, among all the different ones allocated to it;

4- Do not lose the ability, as it is a space-time of coexistence, to promote this same interaction;

5- Do not lose the ability to tolerate other different, ugly and / or beautiful exclusives that are supposed to be allocated in that same space.

It is thought here that:

> "Only where (in space-time) there are different human beings, ugly and / or beautiful exclusive, can love also arise, remain and / or become the supreme value of affirming life ..."

The different, ugly and / or beautiful exclusives are all there:

1- Too high;

2- The little ones to the extreme;

3- The beautiful ones;

4- The beautiful raggedy;

5- Those with very thin noses;

6- Those with very wide noses;

7- The ones with normal noses where big or small noses reign;

8- The thin ones;

9- Fat people;

10- Those without hair;

11- Those with wigs;

12- The very well dressed;

13- Rag dresses;

14- The timid;

15- Extroverts;

16- The workers;

17- Dreamers;

18- The hopeful;

19- Realists;

20. Those who love and are not loved;

21- Those who are loved and do not love;

22- Those who like to sing;

23- Those who prefer to listen;

24- Those who live to work;

25- Those who work to live and so on.

As already said, but here it is still necessary to redefine, in fact it is not who, nor the one who, moved by any objective or desire, intends or intends to be. That is, stress:

> "He who pretends to be different is just the impersonator of a different being, but never a different being in fact." (Artur da Távola)

There are many forms of dehumanization and one of them, perhaps the most crucial, is that which is systematized in disrespecting differences, insofar as this disrespect - in the micro sense - takes the individual away from his ability to coexist and, consequently, away from the possibility of learning, growth and personal development; in the macro sense, it takes society towards xenophobism, exacerbated nationalism, genocide, biocideism, apartheids, socioeconomic exclusion and unilateral and orthodox ways of seeing, culminating in wars, armed conflicts, hatred and radical or extreme political and / or religious positions. , hope cannot and must not be lost, even though, for many, it, the search for respect for differences only sounds like another great utopia. That is, it is still necessary to believe that man can qualitatively transform himself. It must be believed that, as Nietzsche would tell us, "man can be overcome".

UNIT II
CRITICAL CONSCIOUSNESS
OF SELF AND WORLD

THE CRITICAL SELF-CONSCIOUSNESS & THE WORLD CONSCIOUSNESS

Humanizing oneself, far beyond the processes of primary and secondary socialization, is also an act of intellectual emancipation that occurs from and during critical awareness. However, not everyone who seeks critical awareness becomes emancipated, in fact, for two reasons:

1- Intellectual emancipation is a process of transformation and transcendence of the knowing spirit; to conquer autonomy to be, do and remake within the precepts of humanization;

2- Critical awareness, alone, is nothing more than "of" awareness. One can be aware of one thing and not another.

We arrive at an axiom:

1- In order to humanize, in fact, man needs education, but not any education; He needs an education that allows him, through the exercise of his reflective conscience, to develop:

1- Self-awareness;
2- World consciousness.

In this sense, this will not be about the specificities of awareness, but about something much bigger, conceived as the amalgams of the act of humanizing, even if, theoretically specified, aiming to favor a better understanding and that sustain and embody themselves in intellectual emancipation.

I - THE CRITICAL SELF-CONSCIOUSNESS

Away from the radical humanism of the sophists; Anthropocentric humanism, supported by the sciences, in which man is placed and at the same time understood as "the measure of all things" and, even further away from deterministic orthodoxies, whether scientific or of any other nature, one can say that:

1- Man, for being "a social being, a political animal", as described by Aristotle, to be in the world, needs criticism and self-criticism;
2- Whether or not to deny the existence of God, man must understand that he is not only nature, but also endowed with spirit, reason, drive and affection, synthesized in a "human condition";
3- Man needs to know that he is made up of a unit of opposites, that is, of reason drive and affection;

4- He also needs to know that, in the search for an understanding of the whole, specifying and particularizing lines of study and / or research, man was trapped in different symbolisms, in different orthodox ways of seeing the world, crystallizing and systematizing paradigms, which prevents him from see reality itself, but only for you.

5- The man needs to know that, in the search for happiness, in the search for his personal fulfillment, he can get sick, he can have socio-affective losses, he can die, interrupting his life trajectory.

6- He needs to understand that, at birth, he begins to die. In other words, to understand that its existence constitutes a kind of march towards death.

7- In the search for social insertion, he needs to realize the fact that, in society, there are inequalities between men.

8- In the search for a job, he needs to know that he is inserted in a capitalist world and, therefore, also Meritocratic, competitive and Individualist.

Although, at first glance, it may sound like a paradox, the awareness of oneself, the awareness of the "being" about their "what to do human", does not happen only in School, nor only in the family and, much less only in the social networks of the internet or only in other socialization means, specific, related to the exercise of different social roles, for several reasons:

1- In the family, there is a certain layer of protection, up to a certain age, as well as the construction of hierarchies and stigmas between individuals, which prevent them from coming face to face, directly, with the unequal relations of social life and from building an image, a real self-awareness.

2- At school, on the other hand, there is the dissemination and internalization, in the individual, of erudite knowledge that alienates him, insofar as he deceives him, saying that only the appropriation of this type of knowledge is able to lead him to prosperity; better livelihood conditions.

In addition, at school, the acquisition of content is valued and not the development of creativity; Learning thoughts and not learning to learn or learning to think are valued.

3- On the internet, there are no relationships of trust or validity of knowledge, as well as uncertainties about its quality.

4- In the exercise of social roles is the prison of being, stereotypes and stigmas, which prevent the being from being something beyond him, in his time and space.

In favored groups, self-awareness takes longer to happen, since this family protection lasts longer, as well as years of schooling. In less favored groups, family protection ends early, as does school protection. Thrown early in the capital society, a catastrophic reality, implicit in the circumstances of everyday life, is discovered. These social relationships impose the need for constant decision making.

In these less-favored groups, a potential emancipator develops early on, but which soon atrophies, as, when questioning their own existence in the face of social problems, there is no way to understand it enriching and qualitative way, for lack of a solid cultural formation.

In other words, the consciousness does not expand and crystallize, it is specified and limited as an unconsciousness of the whole or as a consciousness "of".

When, however, for some reason, even though he was launched early in the world, by the family, this being still manages to continue in school, continuing his studies later, he has the possibility to confront the knowledge of life with the learned knowledge and build your own view of yourself.

He starts to be able to analyze, compare, question, synthesize, make sense, doubt, start thinking, giving meaning to his existence. He begins to have the possibility to build strategies of struggle and resistance against his condition of social exclusion.

In economically favored groups, this awareness of self, sometimes does not even happen, when family protection passes from adulthood and, to the same extent, the acquisition of erudite knowledge extends.

Erudition alone, far from experience, does not allow the being to develop self-awareness, but to crystallize and internalize itself, erudite culture as being the only way to interact with the world, distancing itself from humanization, distancing itself from need to give meaning to one's own existence. In the same measure, only the experience is not able to make the self aware, but to allow him to be degraded, to have his self crushed, destroyed by social hierarchies, by inequalities among men, internalizing stigmas, stereotypes and limiting their possibilities of existence.

Self-awareness involves understanding your individual and social role. To understand, for example, why, for what and for whom one works, as well as why one studies and what one studies for.

Furthermore, in what you work or should work, or what you study and what you should study.

These types of inquiries are made neither by the family nor by the school and, if someone asked them, they would certainly answer something that did not contradict their own interests, that is, that was associated with money and social status.

It is not being said that the acquisition of money through work and study is not important, but that the acquisition of money should be the consequence and not the cause of existence itself.

On the other hand, the awareness of the contradiction that every being brings in itself, being endowed with reason, drive and affection, would give to the awareness that their anguish passes through the anguish of others, as well as their needs and their needs. aspirations.

In this understanding, social contradictions and social differences are understood in an active way, that is, by building psychosocially and, at the same time, organizing themselves collectively.

Man begins to emancipate himself intellectually when, in his existence as homo "faber" and homo "intellects", he discovers that his citizenship, despite being a right, needs to be earned, as well as his humanization, despite be a purpose of the "being" man.

A personal achievement, when he becomes stronger and transcends his hostile reality; A collective achievement, when it organizes itself for the common welfare.

Self-awareness involves respect for the other, insofar as it is understood that the crystallization of the "I" in "itself" is an unnecessary and catastrophic ideal, culminating in individualism with all its problems.

Self-awareness is the first step towards intellectual emancipation, because it is from there that human beings come to understand the need to question their role, their social function in the world in which they live.

It is also the moment when he can start to see the other under the epistemological bases that he sees himself, that is, as a being who also does not need humanization. Self-awareness puts the human being on the path of humanization because there is nothing more human than being able to ask and ask yourself: ask the world, making it clear to this world that you are alive, that you exist, that you are attentive to him; ask yourself, discovering that you need to think (research, analyze, synthesize, doubt, conclude, conceptualize, compare, answer, doubt yourself and everyone).

In this process of self-awareness, one begins to understand that man is not a human being, but, as Nietzsche would tell us, that "man is a bridge that goes from the animal beyond man". The beyond of man is the "human being". But there are bridges that take man to prisons, to determinisms, to Inatisms, to stereotypes, to stigmas, in short, away from his humanization process.

II - THE CRITICAL WORLD AWARENESS

As the awareness of the self expands, the awareness of the world develops, in a "uni dual" process. However, this second one goes far beyond the mere understanding of society, with its social unevenness.

It also involves understanding the "other", in its different facets; by understanding the natural world; for the transformative actions resulting from the understanding, resulting from the discovery, by the awareness, of its possibilities of change.

It also involves an understanding of the historical processes that led to the culmination of the world in which we live, as well as the impacts and changes caused by the developments in science, especially technological ones, such as their consequences for life on the planet. The acquisition of erudite knowledge in this process is necessary, but also erudite knowledge, for this awareness, is not effective. For two reasons:

a- The history of conflicting relationships between different social groups is not reliable, as it is always told from the perspective of those who remained in power and, therefore, it carries with it a mask, an ideological essence, in order to maintain the "status quo";

b- Likewise, erudite knowledge is disseminated: the paradoxes of scientific development are not revealed, such as its social and environmental impacts and its legitimate subordination to the values of Capital, in its multiple interests.

On the other hand, as we mentioned, the awareness of the world as that which comes from the family, from the internet or from the representation of social roles also does not enable this awareness of the world because, because they are particularists, they bring in themselves imprecision, incoherence and fragmentation, characteristics of common sense and common sense knowledge.

As in the process of becoming aware of oneself, the process of becoming aware of the world also occurs in the day-to-day confrontation of what is lived with what is learned in educational institutions, dialectically.

In this clash, the paradoxes are revealed and the true faces of these two fields of knowledge are shown. In this clash, there is, at first, the possibility of problematizing reality. In a second, this problematization expands and two essential paradoxes are discovered:

1- That not everything learned in educational institutions is valid;

2- That not everything that surrounds common sense is invalid.

It is important to say, however, that the individual's awareness of the world is conditioned by the world in which that individual lives, that is, by the underlying values.

Depending on the world you live in, you can have this or that worldview. We are not talking about the issue from a mere point of view, but from the social, cultural and economic condition of being. Ethnic groups or social groups that are or have been marginalized throughout history, regardless of the interpretation of erudite knowledge on this issue, tend to make an understanding of the world prevail within its sensitive reality and, when known, for its historical reality. Although this is an awareness process, albeit critical, it cannot and should not be understood as a safe path to intellectual emancipation, for two other reasons:

1- The understanding of the world in which we live, as well as the awareness of oneself, dispenses with the development of the self, based on the confrontation of erudite knowledge with the experience of a cosmopolitan spirit that, being cosmopolitan, is capable of moving through differences.

In other words, the individual needs to be part of, feel part of, through his understanding, of a planetary culture without, however, losing his ethnic references. He needs to be aware of the macro world and the micro world.

2- It is necessary to understand that every man, being a man, belongs to his base, to a planetary ethnicity.

Cultural differences between men do not separate them from that base, but only enriches them, from the anthropological point of view. Thus, man's world consciousness must allow him to act, feel and think far from nationalisms or particularisms, but in line with particular and planetary causes.

That is, when man develops a planetary consciousness, he naturally abandons genocidal, xenophobic, racist attitudes, because he also develops the ability to respect and live with differences, whatever they may be. Furthermore, because it is and is understood to be not only part, but also as the whole, at the same time different and equal to all human beings, it can learn from the different and be apprehended by them.

In this sense, intellectual emancipation, as an act of freedom and autonomy to move and dialogue with differences and differences, in the search for the new, is also epistemologically a break with the hierarchical frontiers of knowledge.

Not only with regard to academic disciplines, but also with respect to the values underlying the various worldviews. World consciousness cannot arise from the gnosiological microcosm in which the being lives. In this way, if so, the individual acquires only the "of" consciousness, the consciousness about any specificity and does not emancipate himself intellectually, because his actions aim to resolve the part and not the whole.

Particularizing himself to the extreme, he excludes himself from the whole, excludes himself from the world, as if acting against himself, dominated by the orthodox ideology of preserving the "I", even if unconscious. It is worth mentioning, however, that intellectual emancipation does not pass or dispense with the incorporation of all knowledge, even because this would be impossible. It is a lightness of mind where there is no orthodoxy or orthodox paradigms, neither absolute truths nor absolute skepticisms, but an opening to the new.

It is the understanding that the world, culturally speaking, does not need to be the same, so that people have the right and access to equity.

The awareness of the world, in this sense, also involves an understanding about the "other", about the "not me", about the said "strange", the different.

Intellectual emancipation, as a process of humanization, resides and is substantiated in the dynamics of coexisting: not wanting to be "myself always", nor the "other completely". In other words, it consists in being able to learn and to be able to be apprehended by the different to live, to see the world better, to transform it without, however, transforming it and vice versa. Intellectual emancipation, this process of humanization, begins to occur when, intentionally, one goes towards the other incorporating part of it that makes us even more humanized, better than we can be alone, more emancipated than when hostage to self .

However, without, in the process, destroying our own self, wanting to be completely, wanting to be a kind of copy of it, admiring it, deifying it or having it as our archetype.

But, on the other hand, harassing the other for not considering him as a being worthy of apprehension, for not considering him as just belonging to a different culture, but as an acculturation, pushes us towards our own self, as if our self were a single god, worthy of appreciation and, all others, beings of other contingencies. The understanding of the world, in this sense, has a direct connection with the understanding of oneself: if the being sees itself as something complete and finished, closed, then what is new, different, of riches in this universe of "strangers", according to him, it cannot fit in itself, but only he, his self, can fit in others. This nationalist understanding of the self leads this being to systematize monologues: to always want to speak and never want to listen; always wanting to make his ideas prevail over others; to close in a world of equals, hierarchically speaking; Wanting to be always himself: the same always.

In other words, this nationalist being wants others to see the world as he sees it, and at the other extreme, to be as he is and to share his principles and values.

It is a kind of will to catechize the other, sustained under the aegis of intolerance to the different, to the same extent that it creates for the different, from itself, from the crystallization of the self in itself, the conjectures how different, how the other should be.

Intellectual emancipation and humanization, in this aspect, go beyond the need and the condition of a mere erudition of being, but also beyond only the knowledge acquired in the experience, in the sensory experience of each being.

It occurs from the incorporation of a gnosiological stance between the different forms and types of knowledge, enhancing the being to be able to act and transform the world, based on individual and collective actions, in a more equitable, more participative space-time , because also tolerant and respectful of differences.

Intellectual emancipation, humanization, is an inter, multi and, at the same time, dialogically transdisciplinary way of being in and with the world. It is, in a philosophical and pedagogical sense, although for some it may be utopian, a way of understanding the world beyond disciplinary paradigms, beyond the frontiers of knowledge, beyond xenophobisms, orthodoxies and, in addition to being able to learn from it, let yourself also be apprehended.

It is the intentional, deliberate action of building an ethical, critical, self-critical, anti-nationalist conduct, guided at the same time in the study, in the research, but also in the existence, in the empirical apprehensions experienced, lived, in order, with this, dialogical , pedagogically and dialectically, to be able to overcome oneself, to overcome the unilateral symbolisms of all knowledge, which prevent beings from seeing the world beyond their orthodox paradigms.

It is to deny them: to always deny their so-called "unique", "true or correct" ways of understanding the world and oneself. Both the radical humanism of the sophists, in which man was understood as "the measure of all things", as well as Theocentrism, Anthropocentrism, sciences and other forms of knowledge, led humanity into a labyrinth.

That is, to particularistic worldviews, impregnated with dogmatisms, compared to mythological ways of seeing the world. In the sciences, for example, there is more and more disciplinarization, specifications of knowledge and, in the same catastrophic measure, the absence of dialogue between them. Different worldviews are necessary: the chasms that crystallize and systematize between themselves are unnecessary.

There is no dialogical coexistence between knowledge, but a hierarchy, a kind of epistemological xenophobia between them. To emancipate himself intellectually, to humanize himself, man needs to be undisciplined, in the sense of not being stuck with disciplines, orthodox paradigms of knowledge, abstractions of academicism and dialogically transcending the gaps between them. However, this scholarship alone is still not the path to intellectual emancipation, for humanization, because this path, unlike other paths, is not a gift, a method, but an achievement, that is, it is done while walking . It is necessary that this erudition is dialectically confronted with the sensitive reality of being, with its existence, with its experience. Nature created man. However, it is up to man, in the exercise of his rationality, in the duty to emancipate intellectually, by law and, consequently, by the duty to be free, to become human. In other words, to conquer his humanity, precisely from the moment when, upon being launched into the world, he feels strange with him, goes through nausea, and discovers that the world in which he lives does not have humanization as a value.

ANNEX II

BACK TO PHILOSOPHY

THE WAY TO HUMAN ELEVATION AND / OR REDEMPTION

I CHAPTER - WHAT IS PHILOSOPHY?

The word philosophy, etymologically, is formed by two Greek terms:

1- **Philos**, which brings the first, most comprehensive meaning of love; and the second of friendship, of friend; and

2- **Sofia**, which means wisdom.

Therefore, it can be said that philosophy means, in summary, love and / or friendship to wisdom.

Within history, and more especially, within the history of philosophy, the idea that philosophy was born in ancient Greece, through the philosopher Pythagoras, who, asked by Prince Leonte about the origin of his wisdom, is humbly enshrined replied that he was just a lover of wisdom. Over time, however, in the same ancient Greece, the meaning of philosophy became more comprehensive and began to mean not only the love and / or friendship of wisdom, but also the methodical use of reason (rational investigation in search of the knowledge) as opposed to the so-called mythological ways of seeing the world, which until then were an essential part of Greek culture.

The myths / mythology (Zeus, Hera, Ares, Athena etc.) represented / represent a system of explanation of the world, expressed in narratives referring to gods, human beings, forces of nature, constituted by a set of beliefs, for some fantasies, full of symbolic principles, which, in summary, provided / provide explanations for the universal reality. That is, the myths had / have an explanatory content that does not seek to convince, by reason, the rational conscience of men. In myths, unlike philosophical knowledge, it is believed or not, according to the will, need or faith of each particular human being.

However, the birth of philosophical knowledge, it is important to say, did not mean the disappearance of mythological knowledge, not least because the first philosophers began to develop their philosophies, in many cases, starting from mythological axioms (concepts) and, in this sense, also sharing diverse mystical beliefs while developing their knowledge. Myths had / have the function of sensitizing / convincing / corrupting the deepest and most rational structures of the human mind, that is, to subvert the essential rational structures of the psyche.

Philosophizing, in this sense, today, in the postmodern era, is the same as:

1- Transgress conventional and / or paradigmatic ways of thinking; that is, a way to:
2- Permanent intellectual subversion;
3- Seeking to understand the relationships between the parts and the whole at the same time. Therefore, it is also:

4- Being able to say qualitatively and / or quantitatively the opposite, based on epistemological foundations.

There is also the question of the extent of philosophical knowledge, which we will see below.

II CHAPTER - THE EXTENSION OF PHILOSOPHICAL KNOWLEDGE

Philosophical knowledge, in a short time, in ancient Greece, it can be said, although mythological knowledge has not been extinguished, gained strength and began to encompass a series of knowledge, that is, different types of knowledge, such as mathematics , astronomy, physics, biology, logic, ethics, aesthetics, etc.

In other words, philosophy started to integrate, without divisions and / or specific study areas, unlike the sciences that we know today, compartmentalized in specializations, all knowledge. The very meaning of "university", for example, derives from exactly the same as "universality of knowledge in a unit". Philosopher then came to be understood as one who, while dedicating himself to the development of knowledge, seeks to understand, at the same time, in a critical and interactive way, both from the parts and from the whole, not getting stuck in disciplines or areas specific to knowledge. Thinkers like Aristotle, for example, were devoted to the problems of logic, ethics, biology, politics, virtue and vice, etc. in an integrated manner.

In the history of Western society, during the Middle Ages, this principle of universality of knowledge, including in the construction of the first universities, was maintained, with the exception of theology, which was erected and started to be developed as a specific knowledge or study about

God. During the so-called modern age (15th and 16th centuries), however, with the development of Anthropocentrism (humanism and rebirth) in opposition to Theocentrism and philosophy / metaphysics, this broad concept of universality of knowledge and, specifically, of philosophical knowledge, it entered into a process of reduction, mutation / transformation, as the development of said scientific knowledge, based on the systematization of the so-called new sciences, began to divide reality, knowledge, into particular and specific objects of study.

That is, knowledge was divided into disciplines, specific areas of study, training specialists and, in this sense, philosophical / metaphysical knowledge, based on the search for understanding of the part and the whole, was gradually replaced by knowledge only of the parts, sciences being delimited, limited in a paradigmatic way, to specific investigations of reality.

III CHAPTER - THE FIELD OF PHILOSOPHY CURRENTLY

In contemporary Western capitalist societies, in a process of programmed obsolescence, the processes of specializations follow, that is, each day more and more the specializations of rational knowledge, delimiting their areas of operation, detach themselves from the concept of universality of philosophical knowledge. Therefore, we ask: Today, in the midst of these disciplinarizations of knowledge, structured under lines of study and research through the sciences, what is the real role of philosophy?

Kant, at the end of his intellectual life, making a ferocious and radical criticism of the chaotic world of scientific specializations, which led humanity to a maze, that is, to particularistic ways of seeing and interacting with the world, prophesied in a philosophical tone:

"Men will return to philosophy / metaphysics like the man who returns to the arms of his beloved after a fight".

In fact, not all men, after a fight with their so-called loved ones, for a series of other circumstances, such as pride and ignorance, for example, actually return to their arms.

However, for those who, moved by wisdom and / or love, are able to actually return to them, discover that, for philosophy, today remains:

1- Seek a deep understanding of all beings;
2- Promote reflection and dialogue on the development of knowledge produced by all sciences;
3- Dedicate yourself to searching for answers about said purposes, meanings and / or values of human life;

With regard to knowledge, it can be said that philosophy also includes studies that refer to thematic and structural issues for the development of all other knowledge, such as:

1- Theory and criticism of knowledge;
2- Fundamentals of scientific knowledge;
3- Logic;
4- Critical studies on the paradoxes between the condition and human nature;
5- Ethic;
6- Politics;
7- Aesthetics.

In other words, philosophy today has the function of being able to make the said citizen, as a "social being and political animal" (Aristotle), able to develop his so-called "critical sense", developing and also expanding his reflective awareness from the development of their critical awareness of themselves and the world. In other words:

> *"Philosophy today is the knowledge that must allow man, in addition to not acting accordingly, to be able to also*

transform the world, collectively, acting for the common good; and, in another way, to also be able to transform himself, humanizing himself, and, at the same time, if necessary, also his hostile reality (be it that of a being said to be excluded socially, culturally or any other nature)."(my emphasis)

IV CHAPTER - THE SOCIAL FUNCTION OF THE PHILOSOPHER

As can be seen, following the previous chapter, Philosophy, although many do not know:

1- It's not science,
2- It is not religion,
3- It's not mythology,
4- It is not cosmology;
5- Nor is there any way of knowing that it can be:
6- Canned,

7- Packaged,

8- Marketed and / or sold in the consumer market as wisdom.

In this sense, even philosophy courses, do not train philosophers, but only knowledgeable about philosophical knowledge, because philosophizing is not taught: one lives, one learns ...

In other words, philosophizing is not:

1- Learn philosophical knowledge and repeat it, like parrots; it is not:

2- Express thoughts already thought by other thinkers.

Philosophizing is:

1- By the use or not of all knowledge, mystical, mythical, scientific, empirical, pragmatic and etc. to be able to place oneself consciously critical before the world, with regard to multiple cultures, values, ways of knowing and etc., aiming to destroy and build new values and meanings, that is:

2- It is being able to discern;

3- To evaluate;

4- Criticize; and...

5- Point out ways to social problems, whether collective or properly individual.

For this and other reasons, note:

> "In no ideological, unequal and slave society, philosophers are well regarded, since their very existence represents a threat to the anti-equitable purposes of any established order." (my emphasis)

So, stress again:

> "Trying to disqualify philosophy, while knowing, and derogating the philosopher, as a thinking subject, has long been the role of conservative elites."(my emphasis)

For example, comparisons, disseminated in common sense, of the philosopher as being said are not rare:

1- Crazy; and, from philosophy:

2- As being said, "the thing such that, without which, the world remains just as it is."

Conservative elites have been trying for centuries to transform philosophy, before the social imaginary, into a kind of useless knowledge, which has no practical relevance, although it is not exactly pragmatic, for solving social and personal problems. However, even with all this attempt to abort philosophy, social paradoxes, whether in environmental issues or in questions of scientific knowledge, the need for its resurgence has been clarified, that is, for the return of knowledge, such as the philosophical , whatever:

1- More complex;

2- More questioning and / or critical of postmodern social dynamics;

3- Able to point out ways and new solutions to complex problems.

In other words, the sciences - under the basis of North American pragmatism, in many areas of knowledge - fail to give society rationalized explanations in a complex way and, thus, end up becoming dogmas through excessive specialization of knowledge.

For example, the sciences, in general, accept the evolutionary thesis and say that man originated from the same family as the great apes (gorilla, orangutan, chimpanzee), however, never any kind of experience of this nature had been reproduced in laboratories and / or the same phenomenon, which is known to continue to happen in nature.

That is, there is evidence, probabilities, etc. In this and many other cases, therefore, science only supports dogmas. As we have pointed out, the sciences arose, in Western societies, from Humanism and the Renaissance (in opposition to Theocentrism and philosophy / metaphysics), promising to solve all social and human problems without, however, having achieved plausible successes in the which refers to social inequality, even though technological advances have been widespread in recent decades.

V CHAPTER - ON THE MEANING OF PHILOSOPHY

Philosophy, therefore, is not something utilitarian, something that can be produced on a large scale and transformed, through it, as does the cultural industry and / or the technical sciences, different beings in equal.

Philosophy is what each particular being, through it, in exercising it, asserts itself as the being that it is - in a dialogical process of learning from others.

That is, "learning, with the different, things that can make you better than you are, but without, however, in the same process, wanting to become a copy of the same and / or the same."

SOCIAL ANTHROPOLOGY BIBLIOGRAPHY

ADORNO, Theodor W. Introduction to sociology. Sao Paulo. Ed. UNESP, 2008.

ADORNO, Theodor W., Horkheimer, Max. Dialectic of enlightenment. Rio de Janeiro: Zahar, 1985.

BEALS, Alan. Cultural anthropology. Mexico / Buenos Aires, Regional Center of Technical Assistance, 1971.

BENEDCT, Ruth. The chrysanthemum and the sword. São Paulo, 1971, perspective.

GEERTZ, Clifford. The transition to humanity. In Sol Tax (org.), Panorama da Antropologia, 1966. Rio de Janeiro, cultural background.

BOURDIEU, Pierre. Practical reasons. 4. Ed. Campinas: Papirus, 1996.

KEESING, Felix. Cultural anthropology, Rio de Janeiro, 1961. Cultural fund.

KROEBER, Alfred. "The superorganic", in Donald Pierson (org.), Studies of social organization. São Paulo, 1949, Martins publisher bookshop.

LARAIA, Roque de Barros. Culture: an anthropological concept. 18th. Ed. Rio de Janeiro. Jorge Zahar Editor, 2005.

LÉVI-STRAUSS, Claude. The wild thought. São Paulo, Cia. Editora Nacional, 1976.

LEVINE, Donald. Views of the sociological tradition. Rio de Janeiro: Zahar. 1997.

LOCK, John. Essay about human understanding. The Thinkers Collection, São Paulo, Abril Cultural.

MERCIER, Paul. History of anthropology. Rio de Janeiro, Brazilian Civilization, 1977.

SAHLINS, Marshall. Culture and the environment: the study of cultural ecology, in Sol Tax (org.) Panorama of Anthropology. Rio de Janeiro, Culture Fund.

_ Culture and practical reason. Rio de Janeiro, Zahar Editor.

VELHO, Gilberto and VIVEIROS DE CASTRO, Eduardo. "The concept of culture and the study of complex societies". Culture Notebooks. USU (Santa Úrsula University), year 2, nº 2, Rio de Janeiro, 1980.

BIBLIOGRAPHY OF POLITICAL EDUCATION PHILOSOPHY

APPLE, M. Education and power. Porto Alegre: Medical Arts, 1989.

BOURDIEU, P. Reproduction. Rio de Janeiro: F. Alves, 1975.

THE THINKERS COLLECTION: related to the thinking of Aristotle, Sartre and others.

COSTA, Cleberson. Emancipated & Mediocre. Rio de Janeiro. Amazon.com, 2012.

COSTA, Cleberson. The complexity of the obvious. Rio de Janeiro. Authors' Club, 2012.

DELORS, Jacques. Education for the 21st century: issues and perspectives. Porto Alegre. Artmed, 2005.

FREIRE, Paulo. Pedagogy of autonomy. Sao Paulo. Peace and Earth, 1996.

FRIGOTTO, Gaudêncio. Education and Crisis of Real Capitalism. São Paulo: Cortez, 1996.

GENTILI, P. & FRIGOTTO, G. (ORGs). Denied Citizenship: exclusion policies in education and work. São Paulo, Cortez, 2002.

SAVIANI, Dermeval. School and Democracy. Sao Paulo. Cortez, 1998.

MORIN, E. The seven types of knowledge necessary for the education of the future. Sao Paulo. Cortez; BRASILIA: UNESCO, 2001.

RANCIÈRE, Jacques. The ignorant master: five lessons on intellectual emancipation. Belo Horizonte: Authentic, 2002.

BASIC BIBLIOGRAPHY OF PHILOSOPHY

BOBBIO, Norberto ET alii. Policy Dictionary. Trad. Luiz warrior Pinto Cacais ET alii. Brasília, Ed. University of Brasília, 1986.

BOBBIO, Norberto. The concept of civil society. Rio de Janeiro, 1995.

BOCHENSK, Innocentius Marie. Contemporary Western philosophy. Trad., Coord., And rev. Alfredo Bosi. São Paulo, Mestre Jou, 1982.

CHÂTELET, François, dir. History of Philosophy - ideas, doctrines. Rio de Janeiro, Zahar, 1981. 8v.

FOULQUIÉ, Paul. Existentialism. Trad. J. Guinsburg. 3rd ed. São Paulo - Rio de Janeiro, Difel, 1975.

MOUNIER, Emmanuel. Introduction to existentialisms. Trad. João Bénard da Costa. São Paulo, two cities bookshop, 1963.

THE THINKERS. São Paulo, cultural April. Collection from which the volumes were used: Aristotle, Heidegger, Kant, Locke, Marx, Sartre, Descartes and Francis Bacon.

www.ingramcontent.com/pod-product-compliance
Lightning Source LLC
Chambersburg PA
CBHW060409290526
45791CB00002B/667